HOW TO GET KIDS GARDENING WITH THE SKINNY JEAN GARDENER

MATTHEW BIGGS
BBC Radio 4 Gardeners' Question Time

When I first met the Skinny Jean Gardener it was obvious that he is full of fantastic, fun filled ideas and is the King of gardening for kids. 'How to get Kids Gardening' is crammed with exciting things to do and an inspiring introduction to plants, easy upcycling and caring for wildlife. They'll be learning at the same time, too! Every 'make' has been given the 'thumbs up' by four-year-old Olive - all you have to do is get out into the garden and join in the fun!

SAM NIXON
CBBC's Sam & Mark

Lee's passion for gardening is infectious. This book is perfect for the whole family to get stuck into. Loads of really simple but fun things to do with the kids. What I also like about this book is that there is humour in it, too - but I wouldn't expect anything less from The Skinny Jean Gardener.

ADAM FROST
Gardeners' World

Encouraging the next generation to get out into the garden, has always been important to me. Some of the very earliest and fondest childhood memories I have are of gardening with my grandparents. I learnt a lot from them about growing and had my own little patch to experiment with. It really developed my love of the great outdoors. From understanding where food comes from, to learning about and valuing the natural world. There are so many benefits to kids getting their hands dirty and encouraging them to do this, is something Lee has been doing for his whole career.

I have known Lee for a long time, both professionally and as a friend. For me, what has always blown me away about him is not just his passion and enthusiasm, but also his tireless efforts to pass his love of gardening onto youngsters. We could do with more people like Lee to spread the word.

Horticulture has always had an image of not being very 'cool', but if we can inspire kids at an early age then hopefully the next generation will value the importance of plants and gardens for their health, well-being and the planet! Lee's book is only going to help this happen.

As seen on Blue Peter & CBBC

A 'JAJAJA' BOOK

First published in Great Britain in 2020 by JaJaJa Books

Design, illustration and artwork by Karen Clark, PinkCreative

Photography by Jonathan Ward, Ginger Horticulture

ISBN 978-1-9162933-0-4

Printed in Great Britain

www.jajaja-books.com

This book is for my daughter, Olive, with whom many of
these ideas and practices have been tried and tested.
She's not getting a percentage of the profits from this, so
I'm hoping that this **thank-you** at the start will be enough
to cover me both as a father, and legally in the future.
Love Daddy

WHAT IS THIS BOOK ABOUT?

This is the most cheesy line you will find in this book, but...

you literally have a **whole adventure waiting** for you and the family outside your back door.

The Early Learning Goals
I really think that every child should know how to Grow Their Own before they head to secondary school. With Olive, my daughter, starting school at the time of writing and being part of Early Years Learning, I think this is the perfect time to get them started.

So in the book, for each project, I've added the Early Learning Goals, to help teachers get pupils gardening.

WELCOME

...to the only book you'll need this weekend, for those half terms and for the nightmare stretch that can be the six-week holiday.

When we first go to buy a house, there always seems to be a list of must-haves: a driveway, two toilets (I don't know why you'd need two toilets, but anyway) and a garden. But it always seems that the garden is the most under-used space we own.

It gets to the weekend and we're never quite sure what to do. Even worse are the holidays, when I regularly see people on social media asking:

"Anyone know where to go that is free or cheap?"

I always want to shout:

"Yeah – just step out back!"

You don't need to head down to the beach or to theme parks or big attractions to enjoy spending time with each other. We all know what it's like when we head to these places. The costs add up. Whereas the real adventure is just sitting there waiting for you in the garden.

So, from my work formerly as the 'Blue Peter' gardener and now as a television and online family gardener, I thought I would get all my cheap and easy gardening makes into one place where you can just grab this book and pick a make that you can do together.

There are gardening makes in here for gardens of any size, whether you have a long garden, a small courtyard or even just a window sill. They're cheap enough, so that if you're renting, you're not spending loads of money on someone else's garden; and they can easily be moved to another garden if you like. These makes are perfect for schools and community gardens too, as they really bring everyone together, creating real memories – something no computer screen can do.

These makes cost very little – the most expensive is about £20 – and that's because I don't want you to shy away from grabbing this book and letting the kids pick an activity. The last thing I want is for you to let the kids choose and then you think: "Ah, thanks Lee, now I've got to shell out." Sitting together and choosing what activity you want to do as a family is all part of it.

Gardening should be accessible for all, easy to start and, most of all, something to enjoy and have fun with together.

WHY SKINNY JEANS?

Hey there! My name is Lee Connelly, also known as the Skinny Jean Gardener, because when I started gardening, skinny jeans were fashionable (and still are at the time of writing).

This book (just like those skinny jeans) will no doubt stand the test of time, and so if you're wearing boot-cut jeans or flares, I would probably still speak to you over the garden fence or down the allotment.

My whole gardening adventure – and what an adventure it has been – started with a simple allotment that my brother Dale and I were lucky enough to obtain from the council. The first day we got down there, we just stared at it, with no clue about what to do next.

There was a man – we never found out his name, but let's call him Dave – who would stare at us, arms crossed, not a single word spoken, with no wave and eyes that didn't blink. Not the most helpful of gardeners to start with.

But then there was Chemical Alan, who was the total opposite of Dave; a friendly character who was extremely helpful if you wanted to spray everything with chemicals **(which we most definitely did not)**, but at least said hello when we were down there with spade in hand. For very different reasons, we were scared to ask either Dave or Alan any big gardening questions. Then Alan's shed – perhaps unsurprisingly – went up in flames and he was never seen again, which was quite suspicious, but no one really questioned it too much.

Given that these two men seemed to be our only options, Dale and I hit up the social media and asked our friends and other gardeners how and what to grow. Before we knew it, we were digging over beds, planting up seeds and watering our plants. We were learning through social media, through the people who had been there and done that.

Our adventure into gardening had begun; and so the Skinny Jean Gardeners were born.

OLIVE

WHY CHILDREN SHOULD GARDEN

If you think back to your childhood, what do you remember most? Climbing trees, making dens, playing hide-and-seek. Very rarely do I sit down and talk about that great episode of 'ChuckleVision' that I watched in 1998.

It would be so easy to talk about children being stuck on a screen. I mean, as I write this book, my daughter Olive is sitting with my wife watching someone on YouTube create Disney characters out of Play-Doh. Go figure.

The whole idea of children having too much screen time is a classic PR exercise that is basically solved by just not letting the kids spend the whole time on a device.

Away from all that, being out in the garden is about creating wonderful memories as a family or with friends. When I ask Olive what she remembers from our times together, it will always be the experience of being outside, getting messy and growing together.

So getting out there and creating something is where it's at; and it's my hope that this book will create those 'selfie' moments together that will give you a story to tell in the future.

Then it's the whole magical thing of growing your own. Knowing where our food comes from and how it's grown is so important. I still can't believe that, by the age of 25, I didn't know that potatoes grew below ground. Maybe it's the stereotype of being from Essex, but mainly I think it's because, when I was younger and at school, it was never talked about.

And now I've got Olive I can see even more clearly how important it is. Not only does it teach children this, but it gets them eating more vegetables as they come to understand where vegetables come from, how they're grown and what they're used for.

I always say it's like being a magician. You turn the smallest of seeds into a huge vegetable that you can serve up on a plate. Now that's real magic!

QUESTIONS

What compost do I use?

For these makes, keep it simple. I could write a book on compost and soil types, but I always use multipurpose compost for these makes.

Which seeds to buy?

There are lots of excellent seed companies out there offering a huge variety of seeds. I go into my top 10 vegetables in this book, but not the type – that's up to you. All I would say is, keep it simple to begin with. Move on to the fancy stuff later.

What is germination?

It's that very first moment when the seed begins to grow and becomes a plant.

What is a seedling?

I talk a lot about seedlings in the Grow Your Own section. They're simply the small plants that pop up after you've sown the seed. They should be handled with care. If you're planning to go straight in and just buy the plants, then you don't need to worry about it.

Do I have to sow from seed?

Not at all. Buying from plant in March or April is just as good in terms of teaching the children how to care for the plants and helping them to recognise what each one looks like and what vegetable is grown from it.

Don't have the space to sow seeds?

Try sowing just a few into pots or some of the makes in this book and putting them on the window sill. You don't need masses of space to start growing.

How long does it take seeds to grow?

It all depends on the seed; but you're looking at a good couple of weeks before there's anything really noticeable on the larger plants.

What is pollination?

Pollination is what allows plants to reproduce. It happens when pollen is transferred to the female part of the plant, either by bees or by wind or rain.

When is the best time to start growing from seed?

Start planning in January so that you're ready to begin sowing your seeds from the beginning to middle of March.

How often do I need to water my plants?

Vegetable plants generally need to be kept well watered, especially in summer. It's a good idea to check each evening. Watering in the evening is best, as the plant holds onto the water for longer. (By contrast, water tends to evaporate in the daytime.)

What's the difference between a perennial and an annual?

A what and a what? It took me a while to understand this, but it's quite easy once you know. And it helps when you're looking for plants to buy for the garden. A perennial plant comes back every year. Plant it up and let it do its thing. Generally, it will die off in the winter and then bounce back in spring. An annual is a one-time-only plant. It does its thing and dies off. It can only come back if it drops seeds that will regrow in the spring.

PAINT

GROW YOUR OWN

GROW YOUR OWN

Growing your own food is the one thing that can really start off a gardening adventure for children and parents alike.

I started when I was 26 and I just wish I'd had the chance to get going at a much younger age.

It's fantastic for kids to be able to watch the smallest of seeds grow into an actual plant that they can eat from. It's this nurturing of a plant from seed, watering it and checking it daily, that gives children a sense of responsibility and gets them excited about the end result: the eating!

Sometimes it can be hard for kids to eat their greens. I hear it all the time. Even my daughter Olive can be the same. It's not until they're out there, hands in the soil, growing the plant, that they can see where that vegetable or fruit – which they'll be enjoying at dinner time – actually comes from.

Once my brother and I were on the allotment, closely watched by Dave, we used social media to find out how to sow and grow.

We were spotted by Channel 4's Jimmy Doherty of 'Jimmy's Farm' and asked if we'd like to join him on the farm and help create a kitchen garden.

It was during my time in that kitchen garden that I got to learn such a lot by chatting to visitors about their own experiences and working with Jimmy and with Jamie Oliver. Even then it involved a lot of trial and error – and there's nothing wrong with that. That's what it's all about – having a go and having fun, plus, you should get some vegetables out of it in the end!

I've long since 'moooved' (little pun there) from the old cow paddock at Jimmys Farm where we started that first kitchen garden; but it still provides a lot of what you will eat in the restaurant today.

TOP TIP

Grow what you eat! It sounds simple, but in reality the excitement of starting to grow your own (GYO) can get too much and you end up growing all sorts. The exact same thing happened to me when I first started. I grew lots of onions. Fantastic, right? Wrong! I really don't like onions and nor does my wife. For that reason, I didn't really care about the onions and we didn't look after them – and my Mum and Dad and neighbours and friends were given some pretty sad-looking onions as gifts.

It's the same with children. If they're not initially going to like eating it at dinner time then they're not going to have that passion for looking after and growing the plant. Grow what you eat!

SOWING SEEDS

My three best ways to sow seeds

Before we go into my top 10 seeds to start growing, I've broken down the ways to sow the seeds into three simple ways to make it super-easy to get going.

Number One With smaller seeds such as peppers and tomatoes, fill your pot almost to the top and then place about three seeds evenly onto the soil. Then we do something I like to call the Jamie Oliver sprinkle. Take a handful of compost in your hand, hold it high over the pot and crumble and sprinkle it lightly over the seeds, creating a light layer of compost.

Number Two Beans, pumpkins and larger seeds need a deeper pot to start off – and they're straightforward too. Just fill your pot with soil and push the seed in about half a finger down, covering back over with soil. The larger the seed, the less you put in the pot, as these will generally need more space to start growing.

Number Three Carrots, salad and anything you're growing in rows generally need a lot more room to grow. It's best to sow direct to the ground outside. Run the side of your hand down the soil, release a good sprinkle of seeds down the furrow you've made and cover them up again with soil.

Once the seedlings start to pop up through the soil, you'll need to thin out, which is basically pulling a few seedlings out to give the plants space to grow. Imagine being a carrot under the soil. You'd need a bit of space to grow. So say goodbye to your mates sitting next door to you.

TOP TIP

Water your soil before sowing the smaller seeds as this will prevent them being washed away.

My other top tip for getting kids to water both the plants and the garden is to give them a watering pistol. This is really for when you've grown your plants, not when you have them as seeds or you'll blow them out of the pot. Children love watering pistols though, and if it encourages them to water the soil and care for the plant, then it's saving you a job too.

MY TOP 10 OF WHAT TO GROW WITH THE KIDS

We could soon fill this book with all the things you can grow in the world; but for now here are my top 10 things for you to start growing in the garden – things that anyone can readily start growing for the family. Here we look at sowing from seed, but you don't necessarily have to sow seeds to get vegetables. It's still absolutely fine to go and buy the plants to start your growing adventure.

As well as choosing the right thing to sow and grow, it's important not to grow every seed packet that comes to hand. Again, take it from me and what I first did. I had so many pots of seedlings popping up, I had no idea what was growing and it all got a bit too much.

So, even though I've listed my top 10 in this book, just choose five to start with in Year One and then move up to a larger number the year after. It will boost your success rate in growing something amazing!

tomatoes

They always taste so much better when they're grown just outside the back door. You can start sowing (see Sowing, Number One) indoors from mid February to early March, but don't actually plant outside until the beginning of June when the weather has warmed up. Just keep repotting to a larger pot in between these times. You'll be harvesting from July to October.

peppers

Just like tomatoes, you can sow these indoors in mid February or March ready to plant out with your tomatoes. As each plant gets bigger, it's an excellent idea to use a small stake to hold it up. With both tomatoes and peppers, don't let them get too high, otherwise the plant will use all its energy to grow taller rather than producing the vegetable.

carrots

Bright and orange, you always get hundreds of seeds in a packet of carrots, but you don't have to use them all. Sow in rows (see Sowing, Number Three) around May time directly into the soil. Keep well watered and from July you'll be harvesting your carrots. Remember to thin out once your seedlings start popping through the soil to make room for what's growing underground.

pumpkins

To grow pumpkins, you'll need a lot of room once the plant starts growing, so make sure you have plenty of space. Sow in April indoors, and also plant out in June. Keep well watered and, as the pumpkins grow, keep them off the floor and pad out with straw or cardboard to prevent the bottoms of the vegetables from rotting. Then it's happy Halloween for harvesting!

strawberries

My daughter's favourite thing to grow in the garden. So much so that, one year, I thought they weren't growing until it turned out that Olive was eating them all. Anyway, I would personally grow these on from plant. Buy your strawberry in plant form, get it in the ground in March and you'll be eating the berries throughout June until September. Yum! They're really easy – and an absolute must.

courgettes

If you're growing these, then you (and your neighbours) will be inundated with courgettes, because if you're growing this plant you will get more than you need. Start indoors in April, ready to plant out in June. Pick the courgettes when they're small and not too big and they'll taste so much better.

lettuce

To sow lettuce, you're doing something very similar to carrots – sowing in rows and then thinning out to give them space to grow. It's best to sow from the end of March through to July or August, ready to harvest right up to October, depending on when you sowed. If you sow every two weeks from March, you'll be sure to have plenty for those barbecues in the sun.

chillies

One of the first plants that really got me gardening. As you can imagine, the sowing method for chillies is very similar to tomatoes and peppers and the timing is just the same. Keep repotting as the plant grows. Give it a little shake every now and then; it makes the plant stronger and helps with pollination. You'll be harvesting the hot ones from July to October.

potatoes

To help kick them off, there's something called chitting . It's questionable whether you actually HAVE to do this to begin with, but I always do. Basically, you pop the seed potatoes on the window sill and let them sprout shoots. You do this in February, ready to put them in the ground around March. These are for seed potatoes called first earlies.

Just to make it a bit confusing, you can have three different types of seed potatoes that go in the ground at different times. First earlies should be planted at the end of March, second earlies in April and main crops at the end of April. They'll all produce a crop for you, but at different times of the year.

runner beans

Try growing runner beans for maximum impact in the garden. Runner beans can grow fast and high – a fantastic plant for children to grow and get excited about. Start sowing indoors at the end of March and plant up, with supports, by May. From July you'll be harvesting those beans through to October. A little extra gardening make – not actually featured in this book – is a runner bean tipi. Plant five bamboo canes in a circle and tie them together at the top. Then grow your runner beans up the supports and you have an edible tipi. There's a little bonus make for you.

TOP TIP

Now that you've chosen exactly what you want to grow, it's time to go and buy the seeds. You won't need to use all the seeds in the packet, so be sure to sow just what you need and save the rest for next year.

SEED STARTERS

APPROX £0

Plastic pots! They're one of the worst things in gardening and, at the time of writing, they're everywhere and come with every plant we buy. The biggest problem is that they're not recyclable. If you buy plants, then reusing the pots to sow your seeds is a good idea. Many garden centres now take back the pots, so buy your plants, remove them from the pot and bring them home to plant up straight away, which will save on plastic. Plus, if you look at online markets, you'll often find people offering them free. So there's literally no need to go out and buy any.

Some of these makes involve reusing and upcycling things that you can find in and around the house. So if you're just starting off, here are a few ideas for things to sow your seeds in.

You will need:

- Cardboard toilet tube
- Eggshell
- Egg box
- Orange peel
- Small plastic bottle
- Scissors
- Compost

cardboard tube

We always have a good supply of cardboard toilet tubes. Rather than chucking them in the recycling bin however, you can use them to sow your seeds in.

For large seeds such as beans and pumpkins, just stack a few cardboard tubes together, fill them with compost and plant your seeds. For smaller seeds, create two pots by cutting one in half. Cut into the bottom to make tabs and fold in, then sow your seeds in these mini pots. The great thing is that, once used, they can just go straight into the composter or back to the recycling.

egg-tastic

Using an egg box is another easy way to start sowing. You simply fill it with compost and sow your seeds. Even eggshells can be used after you've cooked your omelette. Again, just plant your seeds with compost. Once you have a small seedling ready to go in, give the eggshell a little crunch and put the whole thing into the ground. Not only will the calcium from the eggshell be good for the plant, but the shell will deter snails from eating your seedling as they hate anything rough going over their bellies.

orange peel

Precisely the same as with eggshells. Sowing small seeds into an orange peel means that, once we get our seedling, we can plant the whole thing outside – giving the plant some goodness from the peel – and compost down into the soil. Or, once again, just put it straight into the composter. It's all good.

mini greenhouse

Being able to grow plants on your window sill is what it's all about; and this mini greenhouse is where it's at. All you have to do is cut up a plastic bottle into three separate pieces. Fill the bottom part with compost and sow your seeds. Once they're watered, add the top part of the bottle (the neck). You now have your own mini greenhouse in which to keep your seeds watered and watch them grow. Keep hold of the middle part of the bottle as this will go over your seedling once it's ready to go outside. This will also make it harder for those pesky slugs to eat our vegetables.

Once they're used, you can give all the parts a rinse and save them for next year.

TOP TIP

Slugs can be a pain – they love your newly planted seedlings – so use the eggshells and the mini greenhouse to prevent them getting close. Other things can help, too. Try sprinkling coffee grounds around your plants, making beer traps or creating a dark and damp area where the slugs will gather, so you can collect them and move them away from your plants.

WASHING UP SALAD BOWL

APPROX £2

Never has creating your own mini allotment been cheaper or more accessible. All you need are a washing-up bowl and some plants. This is the perfect start for growing your own along with the children. You can even install a couple of bowls and, at the end of each day, they can check how much water the plants need and make a competition out of who is growing the best ones.

It's all about taking responsibility for the plants; and children are more likely to take care of their own plants. This, in turn, will teach them how to look after and grow their vegetables.

You will need:

- A washing-up bowl
- Compost
- Tomato & pepper plant
- Salad seeds

step one

Drill drainage holes in the bottom of the washing-up bowl. *Physical development (using fine motor skills)

step two

Add compost to the bowl but not to the top, just a few centimetres off. *Physical development (using fine motor skills)

step three

Plant up your tomato and pepper plant to one side of the bowl. *Communication and language (discuss what you are doing with children)

step four

Sow salad seeds in a line on the other side and water carefully. *Mathematics (counting the seeds)

step five

Leave your new allotment outside in an easy-to-get-to place and look after your mini allotment by keeping your plants watered and cared for. *Understanding of the world (discussing why it needs water and sunlight)

TOP TIP

Make your first Washing Up Salad Bowl easy for the kids by using a mix of plants and seed, then next time grow from seed.

ADVANCED LEVEL

To make sure the plants are watered regularly, you can take this gardening make to the next level by using two washing-up bowls and some string.

step one

Take one of the washing-up bowls and drill 4 holes in the bottom.

step two

Feed and knot a length of string through the holes.

step three

Pour 1 to 2cm of water into the other washing-up bowl and place the first bowl in the second.

step four

When planting up your mini allotment, wrap the ends of the string around the base of the plants so it goes straight to the roots.

The idea is that the string will suck up the water from below and guide it straight to the roots where the plant needs it. Plus, your mini allotment will need less watering because the roots will be able get what they need more directly.

PALLET ALLOTMENT

APPROX £4

Another level up from the washing-up bowl, the pallet allotment is an easy way to start growing your own without the annoying task of weeding. It's done by planting between pieces of pallet wood so that there's no space for weeds to grow. Plus, the growing space is contained in one area without taking over the whole garden. Pallets are easy to get hold of and cost practically nothing. You'll usually find that companies are getting rid of them or people are giving them away free online.

Creating this gives children a sense of responsibility, looking after and having their own vegetables. It's the best way to get them gardening; and when they get home each day they can check how everything is growing.

You will need:

- Two pallets
- Compost
- Plants
- Seed

step one

Find an area in the garden to place your new allotment. It will need to measure at least 1 metre by 1 metre – the size of the first pallet.
*Mathematics (learning about measurement)

step two

Take one of the pallets and use a hammer or pallet breaker to pull it apart and knock out the nails.
*Physical development (motor skills - ADULT SUPERVISION)

step three

The second pallet will need breaking up, too, if the spacing is not right with the top lengths. You'll need at least a hand's length between each piece and they'll need to be securely screwed back down.

step four

Once you've sorted out the top, screw four planks around the sides of the allotment to hold in the soil.
*Physical development (using a screwdriver)

step five

Paint and decorate your pallet allotment in whatever style appeals to you and the children. This is the creative stage where the kids can really take control. Remember, it's their allotment, so let them own it. *Expressive arts and designs (different colours, textures, designs)

step six

Place your pallet allotment in the chosen spot and fill with compost.

step seven

Plant up and sow your seeds in your new mini allotment and water well. *Understanding of the world (ask children about where best the seeds will grow)

TOP TIP

If there's grass on the area you've chosen for your mini allotment, it's a good idea to remove this first.

STONE AND SPOON MARKERS

APPROX £5

It's super-essential to label up what you're growing in the garden, especially from seed. When I first started out, I totally forgot; and when the seedlings started popping through, I had no idea what was what.

These ultra-cheap markers are easy to make and great fun. And you won't have to buy those dull plastic markers you usually see.

You will need:

- Old tablespoons
- Paper
- Pencils
- Glue
- Stones
- Paint
- Varnish

SPOON MARKERS

The spoon markers can be made out of old spoons from the drawer; or you can buy them very cheaply at markets or online. The idea is that the spoon markers are reusable, so it doesn't matter what you're growing this year; the next time you're growing, you can simply peel off the picture and start again.

It's a great make to sit down and do on a rainy day or in the winter when you're planning what to grow in the season to come.

step one

Rip or cut a piece of paper around the top of the spoon. In this space you'll be drawing your vegetable. *Physical development (fine motor skills)

step two

With a pencil, draw what you're growing in the garden. Let the children get creative here. *Expressive art and design

step three

Glue your picture to the spoon. Then cover with a thin layer of glue on top to protect it from the weather. *Expressive art and design

step four

Allow to dry and stick in the soil near your seeds. Once the season is done or that plant is finished, you can peel off and start again.

TOP TIP

Important: don't use a pen, because when the glue is added it will ruin the picture.

STONE MARKERS

A step up from the spoon markers – and a bit more permanent, too. These markers look really great next to what you're growing; and the kids love getting a bit messy with this. Again, apart from the varnishing, which must be done by an adult, it's a really fun one to do when the weather is looking not too shabby.

step one

Collect several large, smooth stones from the beach or woodland. *Understanding of the world (discuss about nature and woodland)

step two

Get the children to paint a picture on the stone of what you're growing and allow to dry. For younger children, let them go wild with the paint and add in what you're growing with a marker pen afterwards. *Expressive art and design (create)

step three

Varnish the stone and again allow to dry.

*Communication and language (discuss why things need to dry)

step four

Place the stone next to your seeds.

TOP TIP

When varnishing your stone markers, make sure it's done outside in the open air.

TOPSY-TURVY TOMATO PLANTER

APPROX £1

This make is an absolute space-saver and something a little different from the norm. You can hang these up just outside the back door for easy picking, or on a balcony or in a courtyard, and it's all brought together by a simple plastic juice bottle.

You will need:

Plastic bottle
Paper
String
Compost
Tomato plant

step one

Cut off the bottom of the bottle. You can use the bottom part to sow your seeds in and start growing your plant. You can also decorate the bottle. *Physical development (fine motor skills)

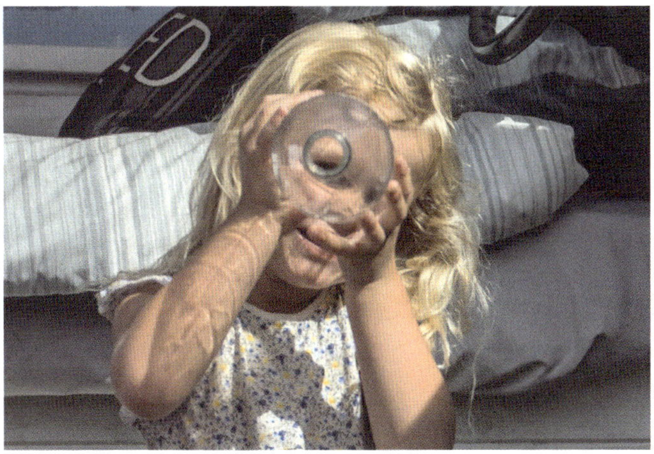

step two

Tie string at the cut part of the bottle so that, when you hang it, the neck is facing downwards. *Physical development (fine motor skills)

step three

Cut halfway through the paper. *Physical development (fine motor skills)

step four

Carefully pull the tomato or chilli seedling from the soil.

step five

Feed the seedling between the paper with the roots on one side and the plant on the other.

step six

This can be a bit difficult. With the bottle, feed the seedling through the neck of the container. The idea is that the paper will hold back the soil.

TAKE A BREATHER – THE HARD BIT IS OVER!

step seven

Fill with soil and hang.

step eight

Water gently each day until the plant is established and growing. *Communication and language (asking questions about what plants need to grow)

TOP TIP

It doesn't have to be tomatoes. Try this make with peppers or hot chillies.

WILD LIFE

WILD LIFE

Attracting wildlife into the garden is a great way to get the children gardening. It does our garden a lot of good too, by attracting pollinators for our plants; and wildlife helps get rid of pests.

Actually, if you can create just a few of these wildlife makes into your garden, it will make a huge impact on what your garden is all about.

You may have seen me present a few of these gardening makes during my time as the Blue Peter Gardener on CBBC (and, yes, I still wear my Blue Peter badge around the house). The frog pond was one of my fantastic ideas. It was during my time with this wonderful, pioneering programme that I began to create these easy-to-develop gardening makes.

And wildlife always seemed to be a winner. From hedgehogs to worms, children love to see nature in the garden; and they'll quickly learn the importance of allowing these creatures into the garden.

In this time of clean, clear gardens, with plastic grass and paved landscapes, we've turned our gardens into a no-go area for wildlife simply because there's nowhere for them to live.

Sometimes just leaving an area to become overgrown or leaving that pile of logs in the corner can really help. These makes will take it to the next level.

TOP TIP

The best way to attract wildlife into a garden is by giving them a home.

BIRD FEEDER

APPROX £3

One of the first wildlife makes I ever made with my daughter was a bird feeder. It's one of those makes that involves recycling a plastic bottle. As much as we try, we rarely go out for the day without using a plastic bottle. It's something I'm sure will change over time; but instead of just throwing the bottle away, bring it home and create one of these bird feeders for the garden.

With your bird feeder installed, you can sit at the window with the children and wait for the birds to fly down. You can then make a note of what kind of birds visit your garden.

You will need:

A plastic bottle
Bamboo cane
String
Craft knife
Birdseed
Stickers

step one

With a craft knife, carefully pierce two holes, opposite to each other, in the base of the bottle. *Mathematics (learning about opposites) + Physical development (fine motor skills)

step two

Thread the string through the bottle. This is where we'll eventually hang our bird feeder from. This can be a little tricky, but you can use a pencil or a small screwdriver to help thread the string through. *Physical development (fine motor skills)

step three

Down near the neck, once again pierce two holes opposite each other. This is for the bamboo cane to go through for the birds to sit on. *Physical development (fine motor skills)

step four

Push the bamboo cane through these holes.

step five

Above each cane, cut a triangular tab pointing towards the bamboo cane and push the tab into the bottle. *Mathematics (shapes)

step six

Decorate with stickers or paints. This is another creative bit for the children to really get involved in and own this make. *Expressive art and design (using different materials)

step seven

Fill with seed and hang in the garden ready for the birds to enjoy a feast. Place as high as possible away from fences or anything that allows predators to get at the birds. *Understanding of the world (discussing food chains)

TOP TIP

I love reusing and upcycling plastic bottles, but they don't look that great; so I always think it's a good idea to get the kids to decorate them with stickers and paints.

FROG POND

APPROX £2

This is a straightforward and cheap way to attract frogs into the garden without having to splash out on a large pond. It's always a bit of a worry having water in the garden with children, but this mini pond is an easy way to introduce water and thus attract wildlife.

I first did this on 'Blue Peter' and then did the same in my own garden. Even though where I live has no real lakes or ponds around, it didn't take long for a family of frogs to join us. They almost turned into the new family pets, with my daughter constantly asking to see how they were. It's a great one to keep coming back to.

You will need:

- Washing-up bowl
- House brick
- Roof tile/slate
- Spade

step one

Get your washing-up bowl and dig it into the soil so that it's level with the ground. *Understanding of the world (nature and wildlife)

step two

Place the brick in the bowl. This is for access and will allow the frogs to jump in and out.

step three

Place the roof tile over half the bowl to provide shade on those hot days.

TOP TIP

Put plants around your mini frog pond. This will help protect it from predatory birds and make your jumping friends feel happier in their new home.

step four

Throughout the summer, be sure to keep the water topped up as the level will reduce.

FROG
HOME

HEDGEHOG HOME

APPROX £2

We see less and less of hedgehogs in our gardens. That's mainly because we don't leave them anywhere to snuggle down and live; and now that we've fenced everything off, they find it harder to travel between the gardens.

Since installing our hedgehog home, we've gone into the garden at night and seen a lot more of our spiky friends.

You will need:

- A medium-sized storage box
- A craft knife
- Twigs & leaves

step one

Cut a 15 cm x 15 cm square hole in the front of your storage box as a door for the hedgehogs. *Mathematics (learning measurement)

step two

Cut two slots on either side of the box to act as air vents. *Physical development (cutting)

step three

Place the box along the side of a fence or covered area to protect your hedgehog home. This is also where the hedgehogs travel in the garden. *Understanding of the world (nature)

step four

Collect leaves, logs and twigs from your garden or local woodland.

step five

Cover the box with the collected logs and leaves, leaving some twigs and leaves outside the front door. *Expressive art and design (creating art using different materials)

TOP TIP

You wouldn't want a hedgehog decorating your bedroom; and they don't want you decorating their home either; so leave twigs and leaves outside the front door for them to sort out when they pop by.

home sweet home

BUG HOTEL

APPROX £0

Bringing creepy crawlies into the garden is a great activity that we can keep coming back to, because once you've built your bug hotel, you can have weekly bug hunts to see what bugs have taken up residence. There are many versions of this, but I really think this is the easiest one to start off with.

If you're brave enough and have the space, you can even create bug hotels using pallets; but they're usually too big for the standard garden, so we'll leave aside the five-star hotels for the moment.

You will need:

- Old pot
- Leaves & twigs
- Bricks

step one

Find a decent-sized old pot that you no longer use. When pots crack, this is the perfect upcycle instead of throwing away. *Mathematics (discuss size, big, small, long and short)

step two

Find an area for your bug hotel. It needs to be away from plants and the vegetable patch if you don't want them to be eaten, as those slugs may take up residence.

step three

Collect leaves and twigs from your garden or local woodland – anything the bugs can get comfortable in. *Understanding of the world (nature)

step four

Neatly stack twigs, pieces of wood and old broken bricks in the pot.

step five

Leave for a couple of weeks to let the bugs move in and then go bug hunting each weekend to see who your new residents are.

TOP TIP

You can do this as a weekend make by spending the first day heading to your local woodland and collecting leaves and twigs and the second day building your bug hotel.

BUTTERFLY FIZZY POP

APPROX £1

Attracting butterflies into your garden couldn't be cheaper or easier with butterfly fizzy pop. In this case, we're making a little sugary drink for the butterflies to enjoy on those hot summer days and to keep them coming back. The sugary mixture will attract the butterflies and give them a place to recover before moving on.

Once again, with something like this you can decorate if you wish. I always think this make should blend into the background of the garden, as the real colour will come when the butterflies visit.

You will need:

- Plastic bottle
- Sponge
- String
- Water
- Sugar

step one

Attach a piece of string to the bottom of the bottle with tape.

step two

Quarter-fill the bottle with water and a teaspoonful of sugar and give it a good shake. *Mathematics (measurements)

step three

While the kids are shaking up the bottle, cut a corner of a small sponge. *Physical development (cutting)

step four

Push the piece of sponge into the neck of the bottle and hang in the garden so that the sponge is damp with the butterfly fizzy pop.

step five

Step back and watch those butterflies join you in the garden. *Understanding of the world (discuss nature and why butterflies are drawn to the fizzy pop)

TOP TIP

Don't overfill the bottle. Just put in enough to soak the sponge.

WILD FLOWER SEEDBALLS

APPROX £10

This is one of my favourite gardening makes ever! It gets the children's hands messy and the end result is fantastic for the garden and the wildlife. Once the wild flowers start to pop up, you'll be inundated with butterflies and bees that will help the rest of your plants in the garden.

At the start of this section I talked about not having a clean-cut garden; and I really think creating these little rough patches of wildflowers can attract an array of wildlife into the garden.

You will need:

- Multipurpose compost
- Red clay
- Chilli powder
- Wildflower seeds
- Bowl
- Newspaper

step one

Put a handful of compost, a pinch of red clay, a sprinkle of chilli powder and your wildflower seeds in a bowl and mix together. *Physical development (using fine motor skills)

The compost will get your wildflowers growing, the red clay will hold your seed balls together, the sprinkle of chilli powder will stop any birds or bugs from walking off with your seed balls – and the wildflowers, well, they're the good bit!

step two

Slowly add water to the mix, turning it into a doughy mixture. Remember, you can keep adding water but you can't take it away, so take your time with the mixing. *Physical development (cutting)

step three

Roll the mixture into little balls on a tray and place on a window sill to dry out. *Physical development (rolling)

step four

Find an area of the garden where you'd like your wildflowers to grow and give it a good weed so that the seed balls don't have too much growing competition. Then simply throw your seed balls onto the soil. The best time to do this is from March to May and from August to October. *Physical development (throwing)

step five

Leave the seed balls to do their thing. The sun and rain will do the rest and in no time you'll have amazing wildflowers that will attract wildlife to the garden. *Communication and language (discuss what rain and sun do to make wildflowers grow)

TOP TIP

This one can get very messy, so put newspaper on the table and old clothes on the kids.

BEE HOME

APPROX £2 - £4

It's so important to attract bees to our garden. They help pollinate our plants and vegetables. As with all these wildlife makes, if we want to invite them into the garden we have to give them a home.

This one is for the slightly bigger garden; and if you're a bit panicky around bees, it's probably not for you. Apart from all that, I'm buzzing.

You will need:

- An old teapot
- Cotton wool balls
- Trowel/spade
- Glue

step one

step two

Fill the teapot loosely with cotton wool balls. This will create a cosy place for bees to make their home.

*Expressive arts and design (creating something with a purpose in mind, using a variety of resources)

Glue or tape the lid onto the pot.

step three

With a spade, close to plants in your borders, bury the teapot with only the spout coming out of the ground. *Physical development (digging)

TOP TIP

Leave out a small dish of water near your new bee home for tired or thirsty bees.

step four

Cover back up, plant around it and leave for the bees to find. Bring in some wildflowers to attract them. It make take a while for the bees to find this, but at least they'll have somewhere to go once they visit your garden.

FUN

FUN

It's all about enjoying the space you've got and having fun.

In fact, in the past, I've designed and built a show garden all about fun in the garden. Many of the ideas below went into it.

TOP TIP

It's all about recycle and up cycle. When I first looked at some of these for my show garden we were looking at spending hundreds or even thousands of pounds to buy these. We're not even going to break that £20 budget with these.

I think to get the kids outside we need to have some grow-your-own and wildlife, but it can't all be about education. Having fun ideas, ready-made, creates a constant activity that the children can fly out of the back door and play with.

It goes back to that question of how we encourage our children away from the screen and outdoors, and the way to do it is to have something out there for them to get creative with.

In this section I have used approximate rather than exact lengths for the wood and other things you will need. Thats because every garden is different, with a different space for each make. It's up to you how large you want to go.

MUD KITCHEN

APPROX £20

I love this! Having a mud kitchen is the one thing that will get the children's hands messy and give them a lot of fun. When I first thought of getting one of these for Olive, we were looking at a lot of dosh, which made me think, surely we can recreate one of these ourselves and add our own little touches.

There's a lot of upcycling going on in this one, too, which I also love.

You will need:

- Two or three lengths of decking boards (depending on how big you want your mud kitchen to be)
- Two lengths of 2x2 wood
- Two washing-up bowls
- Screws
- Saw
- Drill
- Tape measure
- Jigsaw
- Pots, pans & wooden spoons

TOP TIP

Before getting out the saw and drill, design your mud kitchen on paper.

step one

We first need to make the main structure for our mud kitchen, creating a rectangular cube from the pieces of 2x2 wood. Using this size of wood will give strength to the structure. *Mathematics (measurement)

step two

Screw the base structure together.

step three

Measure your lengths of decking and cut to length. Then paint your decking boards in the colour of your choice. *Expressive arts and design (explore colours)

step four

Clad the outside and top of your base structure. To save on wood, clad only the two sides, front and top of the base. The bottom and rear of the mud kitchen will not be seen.

step five

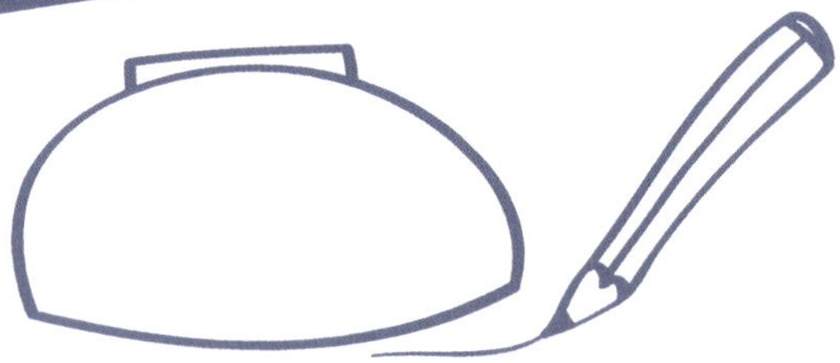

Use the bowls to draw on the top part of the mud kitchen where you want them to go.

step six

Use the jigsaw to cut out holes for the bowls. You may need to add supports under the top, either side of where the bowls will go. *Physical development (cutting)

step seven

Put your bowls in place and add compost and pots and pans.

step eight

Time to play!

TOP TIP

Head to local charity shops and car boot sales to find cheap pots and pans for your new mud kitchen to keep costs low. The ones in this make are recycled from the show garden which I first bought from our local charity shop.

SOUND TUBE

APPROX £20

This make is so simple to install – and it's great fun too. You'll see something similar in children's play parks. It provides an entertaining way of communication within your garden, but for a fraction of the price.

It's like the old 'can on the end of a string' make, but a much more permanent feature of your garden.

You will need:

- Two lengths of downpipe (if you have a longer stretch you'll need another length of downpipe)
- Four L-shaped bends
- One joiner
- Spade

TOP TIP

It's a good idea to place these near a fence or structure so you can attach some clips to support the sound tubes.

step two

Connect these up with the L-bends, the joiners and the remaining lengths.

step one

With one length, measure and cut the pieces of downpipe that will be above ground.

*Mathematics (measurement)

step three

Dig a trench the depth of a spade into the ground.

*Physical development (handling tools, objects and materials safely with increasing control)

step four

Place the downpipes in the trench with the speaking tubes above ground and cover with soil.

step five

It's time to start chatting. It's a really fun communication make for the garden. We even have one between the garden and my office.
*Communication and language (extending vocabulary)

TOP TIP

Plant around each end of the sound tube to make it part of the garden and hide it away from sight.

MUSIC AREA

APPROX £5

Everyone wants to be in a rock band, right? This make will bring out the rock star in all of us.

It's made from recycled pots and pans that you can probably find in your local charity shop or at a car-boot sale.

TOP TIP

This is a really easy make, but you can blend it in with the garden if you want by painting the wood and spraying the pots and pans.

You will need:

- Two to four lengths of wood (we've used baton for this, but feel free to use any type of wood depending on what you can get your hands on)
- String or rope
- Screws
- Drill
- Three different pots or pans
- Wooden spoon

step one

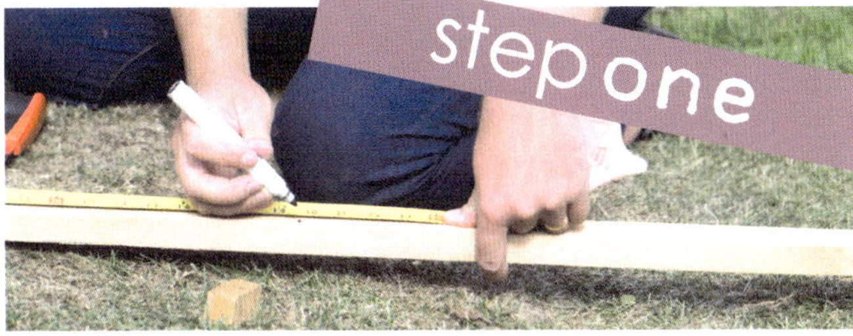

Cut your wood into four pieces – two long and two short. *Physical development (cutting)

step two

Screw these together in a square or rectangle, depending on what size you choose. *Mathematics (shapes)

step three

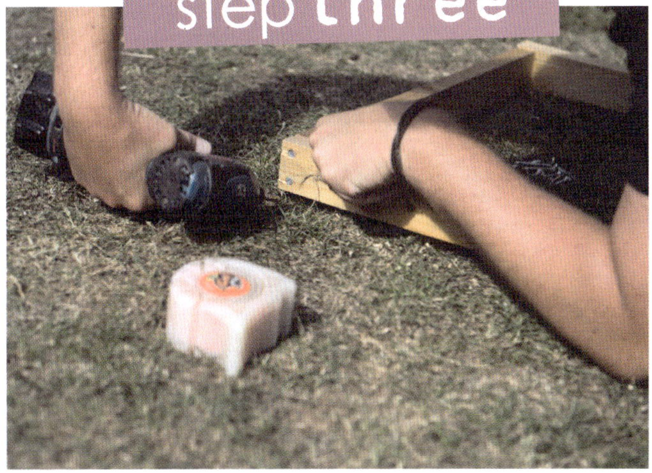

In the top part, drill your holes for the string or rope.

step four

Screw and secure the frame to where you want it.

step five

Attach your string or rope through the drilled holes to the pots and pans.

step six

Grab your wooden spoons and start making music. *Expressive arts and design (explore different sounds, repeated rhythms and learn how sounds can be changed)

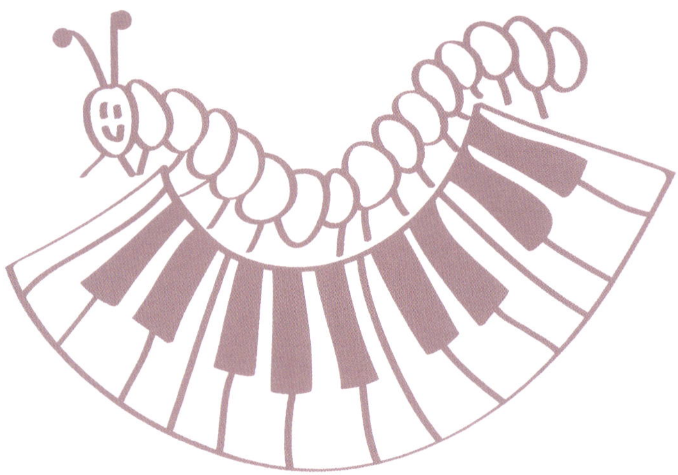

TOP TIP

This make is a lot of fun and a great way to get the kids out into the garden; but if you want to keep the neighbours happy, set a time limit on their outdoor music-making!

CARDBOARD CASTLE

APPROX £5

This is a great idea for a weekend activity or a party. It recycles all those cardboard boxes (have you noticed how some of the smallest of products you order online come in the largest boxes?). It's a super-easy way to create a cheap and temporary den that will keep the children entertained for hours.

A space or den of their own is a key factor in getting the children outside and enjoying the garden. It provides a base that they'll want to keep coming back to.

You could easily spend £250 to £350 or even more on a ready-made wooden house for the garden. This make reduces the cost to almost zero; and you can change the design and space each week. You needn't worry about the design either; just let the kids go wild painting it up.

Let's go make a castle!

You will need:

- Lengths of 2x2 wood
- Screws
- Drill
- Stapler
- Cardboard boxes
- Paint & brushes

TOP TIP

This is a great make for a summer weekend; but if it rains, your castle is liable to fall apart and you'll have to start again. Over the winter, just break down the wooden frame and store for next summer.

step one

Measure out 12 pieces of wood, all the same length, to correspond with the size of the castle you want. *Mathematics (measurement)

step two

Screw the pieces together to create a cube-shaped structure.

step three

Break up, flatten and cut up your boxes.

step four

Screw the boxes to the outside of the cube.

step five

Cut in your castle shape and the door and windows. *Expressive arts and design (movement to express feelings and engage in imaginative role play based on first-hand experience using available resources to create props for supported role play)

step six

Get the children to paint up the new den however they want. *Expressive arts and design (Exploring colours)

step seven

Get out there and play! Don't expect your cardboard castle to handle the wet weather; but do remember that the main structure will stay strong; and the enjoyment of building something new is just around the corner next weekend.

TOP TIP

Before heading outside, design your castle on paper to get an idea of what you're about to build. It makes it so much easier once you're all out there and building.

CHALK BOARD

APPROX £5 - £15

Chalkboards are a great way to get creative outside without too much mess or stress; and when the day is over you can wash it all away and start again the next day.

If you have some wood you're not sure what to do with, this is the perfect upcycle. Otherwise, a fence panel works just as well.

You will need:

Chalkboard paint
Plyboard
Screws

TOP TIP

Have a look online or ask around as you will generally find scraps of wood that can be turned into chalkboards. Or just buy the chalkboard paint and find a wall or fence that you can turn into an art area.

step one

Cut the plyboard to size. *Physical development (cutting)

step two

Paint with chalkboard paint and allow to dry.

step three

Screw your plyboard securely to a fence or wall.

TOP TIP

Don't want to go full-on chalkboard? Just buy some chalk (for £1 or less) and make the patio or pavement your canvas. It works just as well, brightens up the floor and it will all be washed away when it rains.

step four

Then get arty with it. When you're done, just give it a wash; and keep some blackboard paint to freshen it up with. *Expressive arts and design (colours) and physical development (draw lines and circles using movements, copying letters and numbers)

PIANO
DAD

AND THERE YOU HAVE IT!

The 'How to get Kids Gardening' book. What do you think? Has it given you some ideas on how to get the kids out there and have some fun? I really hope it has, and that I've inspired you to get out there over the holidays or weekend and that it really doesn't cost much either to do it!

I have to say a big thank-you to everyone listed here, without whom I couldn't have brought these ideas and this book to you lovely people.

My wife, Samantha who has supported me from the start of Skinny Jean Gardener and has been there for me when I'm stressing and has pushed me when I needed that little boost. She's had to put up with me being away from home and banging on about gardening for far too long, and for that, I am eternally grateful.

My daughter, Olive, who is my number one fan, supports me at my shows and continues to make me smile. She is the reason I do what I do.

My Mum, Dad, Nan and Grandad. They still don't quite understand what I do for a job, but have been a constant support throughout.

To my Dad, who annoyingly can turn his hand to anything and has helped me with countless gardening builds and show gardens throughout the years of SJG. He is my absolute all-time hero.

My brother Dale, who has always been a soundboard and ideas man in everything I do. He is the person that I started this whole journey with and his input has been invaluable.

My sister-in-law, Catherine, not only for putting up with Dale, but also for helping me make this book ready for Early Years Learning.

Jason Goulding, my best friend. He has put up with me since the age of two and I always use him as an example of a general gardener.

The good friends I've neglected while I've been away and working. I know you'll always be just a phone call away. Let's finally go for that pint.

To the awesome bloggers, vloggers, and podcasters and presenters who have supported me from the start and joined me on the journey along the way. You know who you are. You all make this gardening industry an incredible place to work in and regularly inspire me through what you do.

Iain Lee and Katherine Boyle – it was their radio show and podcast, when I was starting out, that inspired me to be myself and go against the grain and to create and produce what I wanted to do.

Jonathan Ward for the incredible photography in this book, and for getting through a two day shoot with me. We've came a long way since the time we met in Japan doing karaoke… (long story)

Genevieve Yusuf, of JaJaJa Books, who has been incredible bringing everyone together to build this book. Without her, you'd probably not be reading this right now.

Karen Clark, of PinkCreative who designed and pieced together all the parts of this beautiful book, turning it into the incredible product you hold in your hands today.

And finally you...
Yes, you know who I'm talking about.
You (covering myself for anyone
I've missed). Without you well...
Did you ever know that you're my hero?
You're everything I wish I could be.
I could fly higher than an eagle,
For you are the wind beneath my wings.

Thank you for buying my book! I hope it has given you the incentive to get outside with the kids and create some real memories together.

At the time of writing, my daughter Olive is four years old. She has just started school and is a proper little character; and yet it seems like no time at all since I used to wake at 10 or even 11am on a Sunday, switch on the telly and watch 'Sunday Brunch' as I cooked a bacon sandwich for me and my wife.

Ah, memories! What I'm trying to say is that time flies. Before I know it, Olive will be a teenager, leaving home, getting married. Oh gosh, I don't want to think about it!

And, while social media is excellent and I use it a lot in my work, having time away from the screen and being together outdoors, having fun, means so much more. Being present is what it's all about. It's so easy to be sucked into the rabbit hole that is your phone and miss out on the little things your children do – little memories that could stay with you forever, rather than who is leaving 'Love Island' this week.

So, yeah, I hope you put the phone down this weekend (that's an order!) pick up this book and choose gardening makes that you can all do together. Start growing your own and create that awesome memory that you and the kids will be talking about in years to come.

If you've tried one of the makes in this book and enjoyed it, I would love to hear from you. So, once the kids are in bed, why not shoot a picture over to me?

Instagram @skinnyjeangardener
Twitter @Skinnyjeangard
Facebook @skinnyjeangardener

Right, now before you go I'm going to plug the podcast. I can't write a whole book and not plug something right?

If you're on the way to work, a commuter with your computer, on a drive or even out in the garden, then the Skinny Jean Gardener Podcast is the one for you. If you want a podcast that you can slowly doze off to sleep to then it isn't for you. Luckily there's plenty of others out there for that! (little dig, wink wink).

Our guest gardeners include Monty Don and his dog (of course), Carol Klein, Adam Frost, Jim Buttress, Alan Titchmarsh, Biggsy – and some unusual ones, including Boycie (yes, that Boycie), Jim Davidson and Iain Lee.

What a selection of gardening guests! All there for your listening pleasure. You might as well give it a listen, but to be honest buying the book is enough!

Look after yourself, look after your garden but, most of all, look after your family.

Much Love

Lee
'The Skinny Jean Gardener'
Connelly

JaJaJa Books

To find more titles by JaJaJa Books go to:

www.jajaja-books.com

Printed in Great Britain
by Amazon

36044001R00056